Prevailing Over My Storms

BY

JASMINE LYNNE FLUNDER

Jasmine Flunder

Copyright © 2020 Jasmine Lynne Flunder

Publisher: Living With More Publications

Cover Design: Living With More Enterprises

All rights reserved. No part of this publication may be reproduced, stored in a retrieval system or transmitted in any form or by any means without the prior written consent of the Author and Publisher. Exceptions are brief quotations within critical articles and reviews.

This work is derived of divinely inspired thoughts of the author.

Any Scriptures were taken from multiple versions of the HOLY BIBLE.

ISBN: 978-1-7345554-4-8

This book is dedicated to my
Grandmother, Annie Brew.
Thank you for always helping me see
the Godly aspect of everything
I go through.

AUTHOR'S CONTACT INFO

Email:
flunderjasmine@yahoo.com

Facebook:
https://www.facebook.com/angel2308

Instagram:
www.instagram/overcome_become_be

ACKNOWLEDGEMENTS

I want to thank my husband, Rodriques Flunder and my three beautiful girls, Gabriella, Arielle, and Serenity for all your support and love.

Thanks to my parents, Chad and Consuela Breeding for pushing me to be better. To my sister and brother, thank you for loving your big sister.

Thanks to my spiritual parents for all your spiritual advice and love.

Thanks to my late Grandparents, Kathleen Mahoney, Carl L. Breeding and Clifford Everhart.

You are the reason I am who I am today. I saw how you prayed through the storms and believed God.

INTRODUCTION

This book is a testimony of things I've been through; how God guided and directed me to freedom and victory.

This book will encourage and help others to get through trials or storms they may be experiencing.

My goal has always been to encourage people with Godly advice. Gods' plans for you are great and He has His hands on you.

Shame

Shame has been my name

Shame has made me blame

Shame has tried to take me out

Shame has made me want to shout

Shame has made me cry

Shame has made me want to die

Shame kept me from my God-ordained destiny

But I realized one day that God has blessed me.

Now, I don't let shame call me by name

I plead the Blood

Shame - get away!

Every time... I Pray.

No More Shame!

My Testimony

At the age of 22, I became pregnant with my first daughter and shame settled in. When people asked if I was pregnant and I replied "yes," - they judged me. Immediately, I felt ashamed and useless.

I felt God didn't love me and He hated me.

People told me that my child was going to be an abomination. I allowed that to affect me and I was depressed. There were nights I cried myself to sleep and wished I would never wake up. I wanted to commit suicide because I felt like I failed everyone.

There was a time when I really wanted to die. I had a gun to my head. I wanted to end my life because I felt it wasn't good enough.

Once I drew closer to God, I overcame shame. In my lonely days and moments, I learned that God was never ashamed of me. He never hated me. God taught me that my validation wasn't from man; it was from Him. In life - God will set you apart even when man judges you.

Revelation 21:4 (NIV): *"He will wipe every tear from their eyes. There will be no more death' or mourning or crying or pain, for the old order of things has passed."*

Jasmine Flunder

The Battle Within

Creeping in the cracks of every corner

Surely casting its shadow on me

Taking over me

Self-Doubt reigns into every inch of my life

I pray but it has a hold on me

Forming a shell of what was me

Yet it is my enemy trying to fool me into friendship

Either I go, or I stay stuck in this state of me
and self-doubt - being friends

But I won't allow it to be

MY TESTIMONY

I had to realize that my thoughts about myself were not God thoughts. I didn't like myself. I hated the skin I was in. There were times I wanted to commit suicide and end it all.

I was made fun of because of the way I looked. This hurt so bad. At times, I wanted to run away. I felt nobody understood me and the depth of my pain.

My thoughts were always negative of myself. I hated me. I went through life allowing the negativity of people to destroy my confidence.

This scripture helped me overcome self-doubt.

JEREMIAH 29:11 (KJV): *"For I know the thoughts I think toward you, saith the Lord, thoughts of peace, and not of evil, to give you an expected end."*

Scars

On the outside I seemed fine; happy, content, and beautiful even

My life starts out as a quiet day

I sit by myself and they walk past me

The dull stare on my face, is this the mark of my disgrace

As I walk the halls of school wondering if they will say something

Do they see the pain in my eyes?

Will I even get a simple hi?

Every day, I am let down

If these tears continue to fall, I will surely drown

Being invisible really does hurt

Wondering if they even care

Will they even notice if I die?

When I am hanging from a tree,

Is this when I will be free?

Maybe suicide is the way for me?

I need to escape the pain I feel

I need a way to heal.

It seems my suffering will never end

Realizing my scars tell my story

I do matter!

They do care!

But God's plans were for me to share my story here.

MY TESTIMONY

People care, they love you, and they want to support you. There is somebody and something in this world that is better because you are around. I know it may be hard to see, but it's there. You matter, and you are important.

For me, I believe my scars have always been on the inside. I battled with depression, being and feeling alone. I didn't feel good enough. I was hurt. I just wanted someone to talk to, laugh with, and hear me out about how I felt. I am still learning that God was with me all the time. When I felt alone, He was there. When I felt I was not good enough, He assured me that He loved me.

Psalms 40:1-3 (NIV): *"I waited patiently for the Lord; he turned to me and heard my cry. He lifted me out of the slimy pit, out of the mud and mire; he set my feet on the rock and gave me a firm place to stand. He put a new song in mouth, a hymn of praise to our God. Many will see and fear the Lord and put their trust."*

Fear

Fear!

Deeply rooted

Entangling

Ensnaring my heart

Freeze!

Paralyzed!

A gasp for air to breathe… to move

And in that breath, I feel alive with this fear

I overcome

I find strength from the power within me

Knowing God has always had my back.

Fear no longer holds me by my hair

I push through it and smile.

MY TESTIMONY

Fear caused me to back away from my calling. I was fearful for myself and my future. I doubted myself before I ever started. Although I was fearful of success, I stepped out on faith. I put God first and let Him guide me.

I was absolutely, completely, and utterly frozen in place. I could not stand. I could not move. My legs were trembling. My heart was racing. Fear, stress, and anxiety were coursing through my veins.

Sometimes, fear is very personal and private. You feel alone. And if you do not openly respond to the thing that scares you, there may not be any external evidence that is apparent to anyone else in your circle.

While writing this book, I've learned that I can do anything. Even though I was fearful, I moved in my faith. Through faith, God has helped me overcome fear.

2 Timothy 1:7 (KJV): *"For God hath not given us the spirit of fear; but of power, and of Love and of a sound mind."*

Insecurity

As I sit on the edge of the bed

Looking at the girl staring back at me

I ask myself - am I good enough?

I tell myself it's all a bluff.

I tell myself as I walk the halls of school

I've had enough!

Wishing I could disappear in thin air

Erase that I was even born in this state.

It's crucial to believe someone loves me for me

And not just what's inside my jeans.

I wipe my tears on my shirt

I am naïve.

Knowing deep down I have to love myself.
How can I allow insecurity to set in?

When God is Love.

MY TESTIMONY:

I allowed insecurity to settle within me. I kept comparing myself to other people. I felt useless. My marriage was failing because of this. I had to let God move in and through me because this was tearing me apart.

God spoke to me in my sleep and told me to trust Him. He told me to love me for me; I am precious in His eyes. In Him, I am beautiful and wonderfully made.

When you feel "not good enough," like I did - this leads to a lack of trust. You don't trust yourself. You feel unworthy and incapable of fully being yourself around other people. You worry about being judged, rejected or criticized.

This paranoia holds you back from reaching your full potential. You struggle with low self-esteem and cannot live the life you actually want. But, becoming closer to the Father has made me more confident.

Matthew 6:25-34 (ESV): *"Therefore I tell you, do not be anxious about your life, what you will eat or what you will drink, nor about your body, what you will put on. Is not life more than food, and the body more than clothing? Look at the birds of the air: they neither sow nor reap nor gather into barns, and yet your Heavenly Father feeds them. Are you not of more value than they? And which of you by being anxious can add a single hour to his span of life? And why are you anxious about clothing? Consider the lilies of the field, how they grow: they neither toil nor spin, yet I tell you, even Solomon in all his glory was not arrayed like one of these."*

Overcomer

You are an Overcomer!

In spite of the Naysayers

The dream killers and all the liars.

You are an overcomer.

You shall walk worthy of your calling.

For God Himself is with you.

You do not have to be afraid.

Remember as you yield all of self to Him

Father, Jesus Christ, will reign on the throne of your heart.

Do not retaliate.

Instead, display the Love of God.

You are an Overcomer through Jesus Christ.

MY TESTIMONY

Even in the storm, we must keep pushing. God is on our side. In this testimony, I went through so much.

I experienced eviction twice and had my first miscarriage. I didn't know what to do. I was scared out my mind and in so much pain. I was losing myself.

Depression settled in. How could I tell anyone of this mistake I made?

Becoming a mom at 22 was scary. I felt like I let God and my family down. God told me that I would overcome all that I went through.

I overcame eviction. And though being a mom is hard, I can say with God - I am being the greatest mother I can be.

We went from having our own place to living in an extended stay and experienced two repossessions. I often wondered if we were ever going to come up in life. Life felt hard and it weighed heavily on us. We stayed with family, but it was stressful. Raising a family in someone else's home is rough.

I have seen hurt and felt it. But the more I went through pain, the more I overcame. The more I hurt, the more I healed. The closer I got to God - the more things change for the better.

I said all this to say - keep pushing! God sees and knows all. He loves us even when we don't love ourselves.

Psalm 103:1-5 (KJV): *"Of David. Bless the Lord, O my soul, and all that is within me, bless his holy name! Bless the Lord, O my soul, and forget not all his benefits, who forgives all your iniquity, who heals all your diseases, who redeems your life from the pit, who crowns you with steadfast love and mercy, who satisfies you with good so that your youth is renewed like the eagle's."*

Faith

We do not know what tomorrow may bring.

Although we may plan ahead.

Only God alone, knows the pathway we must tread.

We cannot know the future

Not one minute of an hour.

Every problem we may face

Lay only in God's power.

It's vital that we have faith.

Trusting that each step we take

He is walking in it with us.

We can't see the future.

Nor the trial we face

But we know God promised Sufficiency of Grace.

Whatever our plans may be

Know that our God has our future in His hands.

MY TESTIMONY

You can make it! Keep pushing through. God promised that if we ask, He shall provide. If God said it, believe it and pray. God never places more on us than we can bear.

I graduated from high school at the top of my class but didn't receive my diploma for years. I struggled with this because a test dictated my ability to further my education. Even after studying, I still had a hard time passing that *one* test. To be smart and passionate, yet unable to receive my diploma because of a state test - made me think I was not good enough. I realize now that God sees me through this hurt that I still feel this very day.

Through it all, I know God loves me. He sees me through all trials and tribulations. I didn't allow a piece of paper to determine my destiny.

Our God really does supply all of our needs.

Mark 10:52 (NIV): *"'Go,' said Jesus, 'your faith has healed you.' Immediately he received his sight and followed Jesus along the road."*

Who Am I?

I'm not the kind of person I need to be!

There are too many problems inside of me!

I'm not the kind of person you'd want to know...

I have too many worries and a troubled soul!

I'm the kind of person who has a lot of stress!

My life has been one big mess!

I'm the kind of person who's gone through pain!

I wake up some days,

And don't even know my name!

I may get discouraged, and "get you down."

I'm giving Jesus a chance...

I know He loves me! Even with my problems!

I'm the kind of person who needs a lot of prayer!

I know that God listens! He is always there!

Please help me, Jesus! Set me free!

May it be Your love that others will see!

You're someone that this person can always depend on!

I'm not who God called me to be

That's why I need more of HIM!

So, I decrease of ME

MY TESTIMONY

Since I was a little girl, I struggled with my identity and not being good enough. Being different is hard because family holds you at higher standard. In addition, there are peers who make fun of you because you're different.

One of the most difficult aspects of life was battling my lack of self-worth and being okay with being different. I just couldn't understand it.

It's important to know who you are!

Gods' thoughts about us are kind and great. It's the devil and our mindset that makes us think negative of ourselves. We have to tell the devil that he has no dominion over us or our mind.

Walk in authority! God has given it to us.

2 Timothy 1:9 (KJV): *"Who hath saved us, and called us with an holy calling, not according to our works, but according to his own purpose and grace, which was given us in Christ Jesus before the world began."*

Grandma

Her Praying Hands

When there were only tiny flutters of a heartbeat.

At Every Birth,

She prayed.

With joy,

As the little fingers grabbed her hand,

She prayed.

She prayed for God's strength.

She always gave God thanks.

She laid her feelings and fear aside.

Family still didn't know

Of her many times of prayer:

For their safety and protection

For their health

For their education.

Her number one prayer was that they love God.

In the stressful periods

When she couldn't find the words,

God understood her pain.

And her voiceless prayers were heard.

Her children moved away.

They led their own lives.

From a distance

She prayed.

Times when the family came together for celebration were always special.

She rejoiced in her grandchildren

She blessed them.

She asked about their lives.

They waved as they said goodbye.

She remembered what they said

She prayed.

Today, if you look at her hands

They are lined and worn.

Look at her knees and see how

They are worn because

She went to battle in prayer.

But from the time her infants were born

She has continued to pray.

How sweet are the praying hands of my Grandmother.

And still, she continues to pray.

Thank You!

How do we say thank you?

For your faith to your call

For all that you do for us

Be it large or small.

The time you spend teaching us His truth.

The studying late to give us concrete proof.

All the early mornings spent pleading in prayer.

The hospital visits to show you care.

Your labor is often without our reward

Still you strive to feed us the meat of His Sword.

So, with these mere words for all that you do,

We are grateful to God for giving us you.

Forever Their Angels

Our Father of Love, Mercy and Grace

We plead the Blood of Christ in this place

Free our children from the evil one

Forever their angels, behold thy face

Spoil the agenda of the wicked

Good Shepherd of the human race

Cast down the lying imaginations

Forever their angels, behold thy face

Bring forth the harvest of Zion

Faithful Spirit, we embrace manifestation

Christ life through them

Forever their angels, behold thy face

Divine Rest, we have in Thee
Prince of Peace, sanctify our space

We intercede for their peace and joy

Jasmine Flunder

Forever their Angels, behold thy face

About The Author

Jasmine Lynne Flunder is the oldest of three siblings, born to the parents of Chad & Consuela Breeding.

Jasmine graduated high school at the top of her class. Because she has a servant's heart, she went on to Medical School to become a Medical Assistant, that prepared her for working in doctor's offices and at a children's hospital. Jasmine has also served on the church nurses' ministry in which she served God's people by giving aid and comfort as directed by the word of God.

Jasmine has always had the ability to write. She has been writing since she was a little girl. The gift of writing, serving, and her desire to help others has produced a piece of work that is healing to the soul.

Jasmine is a wife of 8 years, married to Rodriques Flunder. They have 3 beautiful daughters - Gabriella, Arielle, and Serenity.

www.ingramcontent.com/pod-product-compliance
Lightning Source LLC
Chambersburg PA
CBHW070751050426
42449CB00010B/2426